THE MAD GAY KING

By **Christopher Adams-Cohen**

Published by Playdead Press 2024

© Christopher Adams-Cohen 2024

Christopher Adams-Cohen has asserted their rights under the Copyright, Design and Patents Act, 1988, to be identified as the author of this work.

A CIP catalogue record for this book is available from the British Library.

ISBN 978-1-915533-27-2

Caution

All rights whatsoever in this play are strictly reserved and application for performance should be sought through the author before rehearsals begin. No performance may be given unless a license has been obtained.

This book is sold subject to the condition that it shall not by way of trade or otherwise, be lent, resold, hired out, or otherwise circulated without the publisher's prior consent in any form of binding or cover other than that in which it is published and without a similar condition including this condition being imposed on the subsequent purchaser.

Playdead Press
www.playdeadpress.com

By **Christopher Adams-Cohen**

THE MAD GAY KING was first performed at King's Head Theatre on 3 October 2024.

CAST

LUDWIG II	Elijah Ferreira
RICHARD HORNIG	David Buttle
MAN	Thom Tuck
WOMAN	Bernadine Pritchett

CREATIVES

Director	Scott Le Crass
Producer	Amanda Schulz
Executive Producer	Antoinette Adams
Sound Designer	J Aria
Lighting Designer	Joseph Bryant
Costume Designer	Sebastien+Amandine
Dramaturg	Patty Kim Hamilton
Visual Identity & Title Design	Yence Studio
Marketing & Design	Holly Salewski
Stage Manager	Roel Fox

This production was kindly supported by generous donors. Special thanks to: Mary Blodgett, Terri Miller, Lesley & Cliff Lee, Doris Kloster, Kathleen Schulz, Fred Cohen, Daniel Fass, Debra Spaulding, Robyn R Manzini, Stephanie Moffat, Stephen Norris, Monika Bruegl, Bronwyn Adams-Cohen, Nicholas & Beidi Adams-Cohen, Susan Miller, Kathryn Moffat, Joanna Abram, Dirk Schneekluth, Sahar Shiralian, Micah Heimlich, Dale Breidenthal, Kevin Kloecker, Claudia Vispi, Samuel Douek, Fiona Graham, Hannah Slättne, Tony Graham

Book Design by Yence Studio

PRODUCER'S NOTE

The Mad Gay King was first introduced to me in the Victorian rose garden of my home in Los Angeles in the Autumn of 2023. Amidst one of the most historical years of union strike negotiations in Hollywood, my career as a television producer had come to a dim pause and I found myself disillusioned with my entire industry.

Then one evening, as the summer air began to shift from sweltering to slightly less so, *The Mad Gay King* brought me back to life. In the candle-lit twilight of my rose garden we gathered family and theatre goers alike to witness the first reading of Ludwig II's long awaited love story. The extravagance of Christopher Adams-Cohen's words swept me into a world of opulence and romance that reignited lost feelings of hope and propelled me into the world of theatre.

The idea of self-producing a piece of drama completely independent from the whims of networks felt liberating but not without its challenges. Producing my first theatre show in London, 5000 miles from my home, felt like a complicated long-distance relationship at times. However, the chance to bring this piece to life in a city so entrenched in the medium's history is a privilege that I will forever be grateful for. My shift from TV to theatre has been an opportunity to bet on myself and to push my boundaries as a producer, and with the eloquent writing of Adams-Cohen's to guide me it's been the easiest bet I've ever had to make.

Amanda Schulz
An Accomplished Woman Productions

AUTHOR'S NOTE

The seed of this play was planted on my first ever visit to Ludwig's most famous castle, Neuschwanstein: a neo-Medieval fantasy palace perched amongst the south German Alps. Complete with built-in sets for private performances of Wagner's operas, the castle's opulent theatricality was enough to pique my interest. But when I found out about the mystery still surrounding Ludwig's own operatic death – and the suppressed rumours of his sexuality swirling around it – I knew there was a story here that needed to be told.

I tend to call *The Mad Gay King* a 'retelling' because it's more than a recounting of history. The deeper I got into Ludwig's story, the more interested I became in the pockets of the internet where contemporary queer people were making a myth of him and passing around his apocryphal love letters. The play is based on real events, yes, but it's also about the way that we, as queer people, claim and tell our own histories.

The play opens a year after the king's death, when his mourning lover, stable master Richard Hornig, returns to the spot where Ludwig's body was found at the shore of Lake Starnberg. There, Richard relives their romance. I'm interested in how, today, we engage with LGBTQ+ historical figures like Ludwig who used fantasy to survive – but for whom fantasy was also a way to retreat from the world. I think that's what Richard is reckoning with as he tries to understand what of Ludwig's story to carry with him, and what must be left behind.

When in doubt, I always tried to remember the other reason I started writing this play: to tell the kind of (mad) gay love story I wish I could've seen when I was a kid. I was sat on the train recently and saw two teenage boys holding hands. The simplicity of it was remarkable. So I think this play should be for them.

I'm not promising them a love story that will last forever, or have a fairy tale ending, or even look like anything they've been told love should look like. But at least I'd want them to see this and know that they can make a new world. Be it messy, epic, tender, or rough. As long as it's theirs.

Christopher Adams-Cohen

CHARACTERS

RICHARD HORNIG Male, 35-40s. Former infantryman with the Prussian forces.

LUDWIG II Male/Male-presenting, 18-20s. King of Bavaria.

MAN Male, 50+. Plays: Priest, Richard Wagner, Minister Pfordten, Handsome Man, Architect. Might play a handheld instrument.

WOMAN Female, 50+. Plays: Queen Mother, Handsome Man, Young Soldier, Malvina. A singing actor.

NOTES

LOCATION
The play contains several fast-moving and immediate shifts in time and place, spanning locations across 19th century Bavaria and those within the memories of a mourning man.

TIME
1866-1887: from the third year of Ludwig's reign to a year after his death.

NOTATION
Dash (-) indicates a quick interruption.

Em-dash (—) indicates a suspension of energy, to be carried on by the next performer.

Slash (/) indicates the next performer speaks over the current speaker's dialog.

NOTE ON CASTING
The characters in this play are based on figures from European history, but don't assume they should all be played by white actors. Cast the best actor to portray the interior life of each role.

NOTE ON SET
The preferred set can accommodate fluid shifts in time and location. Elaborate set-pieces should be unnecessary. More exciting might be utilizing the given architecture of the performance space, be it a traditional theatre or historic underground queer venue.

NOTE ON COSTUMES

This is one element of design which ought to be dripping in aesthetic excess. Whether with lush, exquisitely constructed historical replicas, or camp DIY resourcefulness – go for it.

NOTE ON NAMES

In scenes which include both Richard Hornig and Richard Wagner, they are notated as 'RICHARD H' and 'WAGNER' respectively. Otherwise, Richard Hornig is 'RICHARD'.

PROLOGUE

1887, a year after the king's death. The shore of **Lake Starnberg**, *just outside Munich. A plain wooden cross has been erected in the water past the shore. A memorial procession, led by a PRIEST and the QUEEN MOTHER, stops in front of the cross. RICHARD follows behind. The procession moves on, perhaps towards a nearby chapel. Richard lingers by the shore.*

Richard   The water is still.
Slow midday light creeps, soft, over the
thickly wooded shores of Lake Starnberg,
Its wide expanse warped,
Like a mirror.
Just past the shore,
Stiff,
Solemn,
Rising, strange, out of placid water—
A cross.
Plain wood,
Notable only in its insistent, remarkable
plainness.

But how can such a cross,
Have anything to do with you?

Has it really been long enough?
To forget the sight of you.
The smell.
For days,
Weeks,
Months after,
I saw your face on crowded trains.

> Caught the scent of you on a passing stranger.
> Felt the brush of your lips run phantom trails across my naked back.
>
> I thought no pain could surpass it,
> Those constant traces,
> The memories.
> But this—
> The not remembering.
>
> They say
> You lost yourself.
> Your mind.
> They say many things.
> They erect crosses,
> And chapels.
> The more they say of you,
> And do,
> The less I –

Sound of rain in the distance. Lights shift.

> This moment.
> The rain.
> My lungs,
> Burning.
> There's mud,
> Light.
> Then –

Lights fade up slowly on LUDWIG, elevated in a heroic tableau, wielding a fencing sabre. Sound of a rising storm.

I don't remember anything still,
Soft,
Placid or
Plain.
I remember—
Mountains, and
Music.
A *storm*.

I remember –

AN OPERA HOUSE

*1866. RICHARD H enters the king's **study** at the Residenz in Munich.*

Ludwig   We must proceed without further delay!

Richard H   Your Highness –

LUDWIG charges toward Richard H with a fencing foil; he narrowly dodges the thrust. WAGNER parries Ludwig with his own fencing foil.

Wagner   But Sire, it is not ready!

Throughout the following, Ludwig and Wagner parry and riposte:

Ludwig   Nonsense, Von Illies has assured me it is a spectacle!

Wagner   The ASS! His lousy Act III sets will be the ruin of my opera!

Ludwig   Surely not.

Wagner   He has supplied me a painted fresco of a medieval castle atop the cliffs of Cornwall!

Ludwig   Is not your 'Tristan' set within a medieval castle atop the cliffs of Cornwall?

Wagner   My 'Tristan' is set within the deepest, darkest realms of Man's very soul—!

Ludwig   In a Medieval castle. Atop the cliffs Cornwall.

Richard H	Your Highness, my name is Richard Hornig, your man has sent me through –

Ludwig and Wagner fight a path towards Richard H, causing him to duck away.

Wagner	It is within the eternal yearning of the lovers' aching, death-loving souls that Act III of my 'Tristan & Isolde' begins: And that absolute DONKEY COCK of a designer has provided me a painted fresco of a medieval castle atop the fucking cliffs of Cornwall!

Ludwig scores a point, Wagner moans. They reset.

Ludwig	Stay alert, Dear One!
Richard H	Your Highness –
Wagner	There is a creature here which seems to crave your attention.
Ludwig	What sort of a creature is it?
Wagner	A red-blooded sort. Military, perhaps?
Ludwig	One of the General's clipped hedgehogs?
Richard H	I am sent by Minister Pfordten, Sire, to take up the post of Master of the Horse.
Ludwig	What? Another? So soon?

Wagner   Sacked another Horsemaster, have you?

Ludwig   What choice did I have? The last one they sent me grew winded only two hours into one of my midnight rides!

Richard H   (*wielding the letter*) I only require your seal on my letter of appointment, Sire.

Ludwig   Why should you require such a thing?

Richard H   So that I may continue to my duties in the royal stables.

They crash again through Richard H's path, Wagner jabbing his foil past Ludwig.

Minister Pfordten has indicated the urgency of my appointment—

Ludwig   Well,
If *Minister Pfordten* says!

Richard H   The military parade is less than a week away—

Ludwig suddenly stops fighting, causing Wagner to stumble forward and nearly fall. Wagner takes up a bottle of champagne from the desk, swigs from it.

Ludwig   What *Minister Pfordten* fails to realize is that such obligatory pageantry *pales* in comparison to the work at hand in this very room, which concerns no less than the enrichment of the artistic soul of Bavaria through the music of Richard Wagner!

Richard H   Who?

Wagner chokes, spits up champagne.

Ludwig   Good man, you happen to be in the presence of the greatest composer of this, or any, generation. The visionary who has brought us the Dutchman, Tannhäuser, Lohengrin!

Wagner   It's as I've told you! These Bavarian yokels will never understand my work! I must leave this godforsaken city at once.

Ludwig   But Friend!

Wagner   I shall go where my genius is acknowledged.

Ludwig   I acknowledge it!

Wagner   Where my music may incite willing souls —

Ludwig   We are willing!
Incite us!

Wagner   Where the name 'Richard Wagner' is met with pride, not derision!

Ludwig   Whatever you need,
Sir,
Only name it,
And it shall be yours!

Wagner   I suppose,
Of course,
If I had my own opera house...

Ludwig   An opera house? What should be the cost of such a thing?

Wagner   You mean to say the value of my music might be so quantified?

Ludwig   I only mean –

Wagner   So, should 'Tristan' suffer at the mercy of mediocre stagecraft?
Shall I live in a state of squalor, deprivation,
My inspiration left to wither on the vine as a decaying flower?
Bereft of all beauty,
Love,
Pleasure?

Ludwig   No!

Wagner   My King,
I need beauty to make beauty.

Ludwig   Of course.

Wagner   Must know pleasure to give pleasure.

Ludwig   Yes.

Wagner   Be inspired.
To inspire.

Ludwig   I will simply instruct my ministers to open a new line of credit.

Richard H   Sire, I must insist –

Ludwig   An opera house, you say?

Wagner At the shore of the Isar river.

Ludwig I see it now!

Wagner If only your people shared such vision.

Ludwig The Bavarian people are proud, but true.
Your music is the truth, universal, and
therefore it must be *their* truth.
(appraising Richard H)
Why, isn't this the same red-blooded German
your work should strive to reach?
A very 'Tristan,' in the flesh!
What say you, Horsemaster?
Does not this shrine to the innermost
workings of the soul of Man, this monolith to
music at the shore of the Isar River, surpass
in drudgery the tiresome routine of a military
parade?

Richard H It may surpass it in drudgery,
That is not for me to know.
What I do know is, in less than a week, four
thousand soldiers will be marching down the
Maximilianstrasse.
It will be up to me to ensure that all the
horses in the stable are well-trained and fed,
That all equipment is in good condition,
That the troops have been properly briefed,
outfitted, drilled.
They—along with thousands of personnel
across the city—
Will be depending upon the machinery of
this parade to run efficiently,

Smoothly.
And that is also my responsibility,
A responsibility I do not take lightly.
For though it may be drudgery,
It is also their livelihood.
The thing by which they survive,
Amidst rising taxes,
And landlords,
The threat of draught.
And if I am not allowed to do my job,
If I am not allowed to get down to the stables
Now,
to take stock of the state of things and take decisive action,
If I am made to let these people down,
I must admit,
Sire,
I do somehow doubt an opera house will be of much consolation to them.

Wagner stares with his mouth agape. After a moment, Richard H slams the letter on the desk and moves to storm towards the exit. Ludwig blocks his path. He takes the letter, places his seal upon it, and hands it back to him. Richard H exits.

HE IS OUR KING

MINISTER PFORDTEN and the QUEEN MOTHER appear in spots.

Queen Mother	And if my son's tastes are rather more extravagant than those of my late husband? So be it! He is our king.
Pfordten	Treasury spending has nearly *quadrupled* since he took the throne. And with our country at the precipice of war –
Queen Mother	Do refrain, Minister, from discussing such unbefitting topics in my presence.
Pfordten	But Madam –
Queen Mother	We have more pressing concerns… I am told there is a new man at the stables.
Pfordten	I—
Queen Mother	A dashing, blue-eyed Prussian.
Pfordten	Yes, Madam.
Queen Mother	Ever since his dear cousin the Count von Thurn und Taxis was married, the king has been starved for a friend. Someone with whom to share his manly spirit: for climbing, for the outdoors, for – well, you know how young men are.
Pfordten	Quite.

Queen Mother It is said my son has taken a liking to this new Horsemaster.

Pfordten I must admit, I fail to see how such a matter warrants the attention of the Council of Ministers.

Queen Mother I am no statesman. And yet it seems evident—even to me—that any politically-minded man would do *well* to keep track of his king's noted new favourites.

Pfordten There *are* intimacies such a confidant has access to which might be of interest to the council…

Queen Mother Indeed, it seems to me that any man who should succeed in *closely* and *discreetly* managing his king's private affairs, in ensuring the influence of certain parties does not keep him from his duties to the royal house… Why, such a man should have no difficulty in managing any position within the council he so desired.

Pfordten Even unto the office of Prime Minister…?

Queen Mother The *details* of diplomacy are unsuited to my station, Sir. Still, I see no reason a man of decent political ideals shouldn't profit from looking after the interests of the monarchy.

Pfordten It is said the king has taken a liking to the new Horsemaster…? Such confidences might indeed be a boon to the royal house. Granted they are, as you say, *managed*.

Queen Mother Even a monarch needs friends.

Pfordten And how rare it is, Madam, to find a true friend within the court.

WE RIDE

*That night. In the **servant's quarters**. RICHARD is shirtless: a bandage is wrapped about his shoulder and chest. LUDWIG appears, in shadow, at the door to his room.*

Ludwig I want you to take me.

Richard Your Highness—?

Ludwig Tomorrow,
At the borderlands,
Our allies in the German Confederation will face Bismarck's troops.
I want you to take me.

Richard Into battle?

Ludwig You think that I am foolish. Frivolous...
I am expected, at next week's military parade, to send troops to aid our allies in this civil war. How can I know what's at stake, to break this country's fifty-year peace, with nothing but Minister Pfordten's infernal postulations to go by?

Richard Sire –

Ludwig You served. First Lieutenant Richard Hornig. Honourably discharged after receiving injury in battle.

He eyes Richard's bandage. Richard replaces his shirt.

I was eighteen when I succeeded my father to the throne. I never trained with our

	forces, as my brother Otto has. Have never seen battle. How can I lead my country into war, when everything I know of it has come from books and tutors? Parades. I want you to take me. To see.
Richard	You won't like what you see.
Ludwig	To know. *(moving to leave)* Hitch up the horses.
Richard	It's the middle of the night.
Ludwig	The moon is in Scorpio.
Richard	Your Highness –
Ludwig	We ride tonight.

Ludwig exits. Lights shift.

Richard	In the stables, the horses are hot. Orion whinnies, bucks— steam rising from her nostrils into the cold night air and snaking around me like some bad omen. 'Easy Girl.' I ease my hand over the strong curve of her back, Urging her forward, Cooling her blood, Willing her to my command.

Ludwig appears, in riding costume.

Ludwig	We ride!

They ride.

Richard We ride through the night, from Munich towards Münchengratz—

Ludwig On, Galahad!
On, Percival!

Richard Never breaking, not even for a moment's rest.

Ludwig To reach Avalon, we must outrun the day!

Richard I don't look back.

Ludwig We must never look back!

Richard I know the way.
I push on.

WARM BROTHERS

*LUDWIG and RICHARD have arrived just outside the battleground at Münchengratz, to wait out the small hours in the **drinking hall of a boarding house**. Sexy music plays as HANDSOME MEN in lederhosen dance together. Ludwig, wearing a workman's uniform and hat as disguise, hands Richard a stein of beer.*

Richard They seem to know you here.

Ludwig *(referring to his disguise)* They know 'Hans,' the sugar beet farmer...

Richard They know Hans, then.

Ludwig On long nights, when evening rides stretch into strange country terrain, such establishments, and the warm brothers within them, have been my refuge. Take a look around you. At the farmer, the merchant, the woodcutter. They are the heart and soul of this land. The young, golden men of Bavaria.

Ludwig toasts a passer-by.

Richard Yes, you appear to be quite popular amongst the young, golden men of Bavaria.

Ludwig Does it disturb you?

Richard What?

Ludwig My popularity amongst them. Do you find it shocking?

Richard   What's it to me?

Ludwig   That is the question, isn't it, Hornig?

Music changes. Ludwig extends a hand.

You aren't going to make me dance alone, are you?

Richard   Is this wise?

Ludwig   We'll be friends. Won't we…?
One dance. Come.

Richard   Only on the condition that I may lead. Sire.

Ludwig   As you will, Hornig.

Richard takes Ludwig's hand. He leads him in a steamy partner's dance across the floor.

Not bad! I suspected you were a man of the world.

Richard   I've not travelled broadly.

Ludwig   Yet you've a studied technique.

Richard   Some things come to a man naturally—
(turning Ludwig)
I'm sure you'd concede.

Ludwig   Still, I shouldn't wonder a handsome Prussian officer hasn't had his fair share of dancing partners.

Richard We're not all of us as precociously light on our feet as His Most Revered Majesty.

Richard dips Ludwig.

Ludwig You've had a few, at least. One or two – unless – *(giving a faux gasp)* Oh, Hornig, You're an *initiate!*

Richard No, I –

Ludwig Don't be embarrassed, dear man, it's alright if you lack experience –

Richard *(breaking away)* Did I say I lack experience?

Ludwig I only presumed –

Richard *(viciously)* You presume too much. You're overfamiliar. It isn't a quality befitting a king… I – apologize, Your Highness, I –

Ludwig I wasn't trying to –

Richard Can we just –

Ludwig I only meant –

Richard Can we drop it?
Please…

Ludwig *(mimes dropping something)*

Richard sits at the bar, orders another drink. Ludwig hovers behind him.

Ludwig Hornig.
How did it happen?

>   Your—*(he indicates his own chest)*

Richard   Bullet. Passed through my right arm and breast and lodged in my back, I was lucky they were able to extract it in triage. No anaesthetic.

Ludwig   Christ.

Richard   Hurt like fuck.

Ludwig   But did it happen in battle?

Richard falls silent. Sensing he's hit a nerve, Ludwig changes tact.

>   Shall we make a bet?

Ludwig takes up a full stein of beer.

>   I'll bet you I can hold my stein up longer than you can.

Richard   Steinholding? Are we teenagers?

Ludwig   You're telling me you never play drinking games? Never?

Richard   Besides, it's not a fair fight, your arms are puny.

Ludwig   I'm stronger than I look.

Richard   I'd crush you, Sire. No offense.

Ludwig   Come, I'll bet you Orion's saddle I can hold it out longer than you can.

Richard	And if you win?
Ludwig	You tell me your story.

Richard stands, takes up his stein.

Richard	Ready?
Ludwig	Set—

They hold their steins straight out in front of them perpendicular to the floor. Ludwig's arm starts shaking.

Richard	It'll be a sad day when the great King Ludwig II loses so miserably to a mere equerry.
Ludwig	What, so suddenly competitive, man?
Richard	You asked for it.
Ludwig	Did I?
Richard	Been asking for it all night. That saddle's as good as mine.

Ludwig shakes harder.

	I know the look of a man about to drop his stein. You can still forfeit, save yourself the embarrassment.
Ludwig	Never –
Richard	Come on, this is a bloodbath. Surrender –
Ludwig	Won't –

Richard SURRENDER.

Ludwig shakes uncontrollably, drops his stein.

Ludwig GAH!

Richard *(doing a laddish victory dance)*
I WIN.
YOU LOSE.
THE SADDLE IS MINE.

Ludwig *(shaking Richard's hand)* You won it, fair and square.

Richard *(realizing)* You knew you'd lose.

Ludwig Come to think of it, I was always pretty shit at Steinholding.

Richard Then why take such a risky bet?

Ludwig smiles.

I'm still not telling any stories.

A handsome man in lederhosen passes, offering his hand to Ludwig for a dance. He takes it.

Wait.

Ludwig dismisses the man.

I wanted to say – about this morning –
It's—
Normally I can control it.
But sometimes this—thing—rises hot, like bile, inside, and—

| | Well, this morning I –
I lost control. That's all. |
|---|---|
| **Ludwig** | It would appear you've begun to regain it.
(with sudden mischief)
Hey – wanna see something funny? |

Ludwig removes his hat, unbuttons the shirt of his disguise.

Richard	*(panicked, 'this is my responsibility')* What are you doing, they'll recognize you –
Ludwig	Exactly. Let's see if we can't get them to start a riot!

He moves to stand up on the bar; Richard grabs his arm.

| | Don't tell me you're afraid—!
What!
Why are you looking at me like that? |
|---|---|
| **Richard** | Like? |
| **Ludwig** | Like I'm a misbehaved schoolboy and I need to be spanked. |
| **Richard** | Christ! |
| **Ludwig** | Well? We *are* friends, aren't we, Hornig? |
| **Richard** | You know, I wouldn't swear you aren't *completely* mad – |

Ludwig kisses Richard, who releases his grip, stunned. Ludwig jumps up onto the bar.

Ludwig	Another round of drinks!

>>For everyone!
>>On decree of the MAD KING!

The crowd goes fucking wild.

BATTLE OF ANGELS

*The next morning. LUDWIG and RICHARD arrive at **a cliff** overlooking the battleground at Münchengrätz. Ludwig washes his face in a steam. Richard slugs his flask.*

Ludwig (*taking a vigorous breath*) Mountain air! It does a man good!
…
I must thank you, Hornig. To be here, in the face of such majesty—at daybreak, between the steep falls of the valley at Münchengrätz! It's as if suddenly I were a man of valiant action! Not a monarch, sequestered at the Residenz, but here, in the drum of it. And on the horizon—a great battle to be waged!

Richard We shouldn't be here.

Ludwig Haven't you heard me?
…
I feel as if I were on the precipice of some sacred wisdom, I thank you!

Richard There's still time –

Ludwig Enough.

Richard We can still turn back.

Ludwig ENOUGH.
You will stand down,
You will hold your tongue,
You will not let my familiarity nor my
benevolent nature disabuse you of the fact

                    that I am your Infallible, your True and
                    Sovereign KING.

*They stand close, tense. Sound of **Wagnerian Horns** in the distance. Ludwig turns, suddenly nervy. Richard moves close to the edge of the cliff, looking out over the battleground below.*

                    What do you see?

Richard   A cloud of black dust, rising up over the
                    mountains—
                    And below,
                    In the woods,
                    Something's kicking up the dust—
                    Horses.

Ludwig   And men on horseback.
                    Broad-shouldered, with gleaming buttons
                    and silver bayonets—

Richard & Ludwig Cavalry.

Richard   Barricading the copse,
                    Enemy battalions huddle close in narrow
                    trenches,
                    Sound of tense breath in their ears as the
                    cavalry narrows in,
                    Fingers twitching on the triggers of their
                    breech-loaded barrels.

Ludwig   Holding fast to the thick leather of his reign,
                    A soldier bounds,
                    Manoeuvres,
                    Thick arm tensing against the muscles of his
                    sweat-flecked beast—

Richard   3000 Meters.

Ludwig   Green,
                    Gold,
                    Pushing hard across the field into the morning frost,
                    He flies ahead of his brothers,
                    Breaking formation as if to lead the charge.
                    The flash of his hair glints gold beneath his helmet,
                    His eyes burn blue against a valley of green—

Richard   2000 Meters.

Ludwig   Thighs braced to the polished leather of his saddle,
                    Our hero vaults over cracked earth—

Richard   1600 Meters.

Ludwig   He reaches down, past the sharp cut of his jacket—

Richard   1200 Meters.

Ludwig   Raises his rifle—

Richard   1000 Meters.

Ludwig & Richard Crack.

Richard   In the trenches,
                    Men lock their aim on the approaching cavalry now firmly in their line of fire.
                    They pull—

Ludwig & Richard Crack.

Richard   — open the neck of the barrel,
Load,
Reload,
Pull—

Ludwig & Richard Crack.

Richard   A storm of bullets.

Ludwig   Red—

Richard   A hail of bullets.

Ludwig   Hot metal—
Smoke—

Richard   Smell of powder—

Ludwig   Taste of metal—
Red.
Our hero—

Richard   His horse buckles under,
Hurtling forward onto snow-powdered earth—

Ludwig   Slashes of red on white—

Richard   The weight of her crushes—

Ludwig   Bones—

Richard   Broken
Shattered by shrapnel
Bullets rip through tissue,

	He hurtles across the ground like tattered burlap ripped and torn at ragged seams –
Ludwig	Slashes.
Richard	Shatters. Fragments. Heavy bleeding and disjointed limbs. Man after man—
Ludwig	Please –
Richard	*Row after row* of cavalry man meets wall of blasted metal, Broken bodies, Piled, mounting, muddied, As from the trenches, Endless rain of fire.
Ludwig	Men—
Richard	Crawling up from the trenches—
Ludwig	Men—
Richard	Impaled on the sharp thrusts of bayonets—
Ludwig	Both sides—
Richard	Desperately grasping, fighting blind through the heat of –
Ludwig	Smoke. Scorched earth.
Richard	Laid to waste in the heat of –

Ludwig & Richard War.

Ludwig   The forces keep charging—

Richard   Gasping –
                  Trembling –
                  Pain in my head –

Ludwig   Forces ever charging—

Richard   pain in my head pain in my stomach pain in my chest make it stop MAKE IT STOP

There is a flash, an explosion, ringing, smoke. A YOUNG SOLDIER emerges from the smoke; Richard reaches out towards him.

                ERNST!!

Richard lunges towards the edge of the cliff—

Ludwig   HORNIG!!

Ludwig restrains Richard, pulling him back from the ledge. Richard grasps his chest in pain, sobs, collapses into Ludwig's arms like a Pietà.

NOT ALONE

MINISTER PFORDTEN and the QUEEN MOTHER appear in spots.

Pfordten It is not unusual, Madam, for the king – of his own volition! – to indulge in one of his midnight rides.

Queen Mother And is it *usual*, on such occasions, that his ministers should be so ignorant as to their monarch's whereabouts? So *incompetent* as to allow the *heir to the Wittelsbach name* to gallivant about the Bavarian backwoods – amongst the rustics! – without so much as an armed brigade as protection? My child! Alone in the wilderness!

Pfordten He is not alone.

Queen Mother He – he is –

Pfordten Not alone. Of *that* I am certain.

Queen Mother Minister.

Pfordten The king will be here in time for the parade. I am sure of it.

Queen Mother Pray.
For your own sake,
For the future of your life at this court,
PRAY that he is.

FLESH

*Back at the **boarding house**. Ludwig attends the wound on Richard's chest, which has reopened.*

Richard   We were kids,
Just kids when we—
We trained together.
Me and Ernst.
…
He'd help me.
I was stronger than him,
Physically
But—
If I lost my nerve,
Or stumbled,
He was there:
'I'm not leaving you behind.'
He was like that.
Had this –
Unshakeable belief.
'I'm not leaving you behind.'
And when he said it, you believed it.
Most of us, we'd joined up for a bed, a hot meal, but him –
It was like he was fighting for something.
Something that mattered.
(indicating his chest)
When it happened –

Ludwig rinses the wound. Richard cries out, grips Ludwig's hand.

Routine,

It was routine,
only this time
...
Smoke
Shouts
Fire.
An ambush.
They were on us before we breached the
defensive wall – then,
A sudden blast brought down the wall,
trapped half our squadron beneath it.
I turned to him –
To Ernst.
I turned to him.
'Fall back!'
There was time.
Still time.
I turned to him – but –
He made for the blasted rubble,
Towards the shouts of our men trapped
beneath the wreckage of the wall.
That's when –
Sudden shock.
Tight pressure.
Then – agony – absolute – so that I blacked
out, only waking in bleary starts to know I'd
been dragged by a backup unit to triage –
And Ernst
Made it as far as the collapsed wall.
Even pulled some men from the rubble,
before
...

> I can still remember how close he was.
> Shoulder pressed to mine.
> How easy it would've been to
> grab him.
> To hold him.
> To refuse to let him go.
> If I'd only –
> held him faster.
> If I'd only –

Ludwig touches the exposed flesh of Richard's shoulder. He recoils.

Ludwig   It's –

Richard   *(close to tears)*
　　　　　Hideous.

Ludwig   Richard.

Richard   I'm –

Ludwig   Soft.
　　　　　Still, soft.

Richard   Haven't been –

Ludwig   Touched?
　　　　　Here.
　　　　　(inching towards Richard's scar)
　　　　　Or there?

Richard   Not since –

Ludwig   Here, soft.
　　　　　And there

Richard	I haven't been—
Ludwig	And I've never—
Richard	But I thought…
Ludwig	Not like this.
Richard	Never like?
Ludwig	This. So –
Richard	(tensing) Soft. Still.

Ludwig traces the scar, from the top of Richard's collarbone, down to the centre of his chest. Richard turns to face Ludwig. They kiss, passionately; they make love on the boarding house floor.

A KING SO OVERRULED

MINISTER PFORDTEN and the QUEEN MOTHER appear in spots.

Pfordten It's – unthinkable!

Queen Mother Unprecedented!

Pfordten An affront!

Queen Mother A scandal!

Pfordten That a monarch –

Queen Mother A Wittelsbach!

Pfordten Should so boldly, so, so –

Queen Mother So openly!

Pfordten So flagrantly!

Queen Mother Oh.

Pfordten And with such a *blatant* disregard for *established convention* –

Queen Mother Oh!!

*LUDWIG stands now, attended by RICHARD, before a formal committee at **the Residenz**.*

Pfordten Your Majesty. That a King should *oppose* his own government's stance in a matter of such diplomatic importance is unthinkable. To abandon our Austrian allies, to delay any further in sending them aid—

Ludwig	And what of our brothers in Prussia? My uncle, our cousins at the Prussian court? And what of our own men, Minister?
Pfordten	Your Majesty –
Ludwig	I have seen the effects of this alliance, this *German Confederation* and its brand of so-called diplomacy. I have seen, smelled, tasted. What would you have me tell them? The families of our men, after the violent tide of war has wrest them from this, their beloved Bavaria? No, Minister, my mind is made up. We shall deploy no troops.
Pfordten	Very well. Then, we ally ourselves with Bismarck and the Prussian cause.
Ludwig	No –
Pfordten	So, to the German Confederation and the Austrians.
Ludwig	No!
Pfordten	Which is it, Your Majesty?
Ludwig	We shall remain neutral.

Pfordten laughs.

You will compose yourself, Minister!

Pfordten Perhaps my King has forgotten the pledge his government made to the confederation, which to turn against should be as good as declaring a formal alliance with Bismarck.

Ludwig	We shall draft a formal letter condemning the Prussian cause.
Pfordten	A letter! And so, we pit our paltry forces against the towering military power of the Prussians on the hopes of our council's penmanship!
Ludwig	I will not allow my country to enter into war!
Pfordten	Your country? Will lie in total wreckage should you fail to aid the confederation –
Ludwig	Minister—!
Pfordten	And, failing to act, your people will turn against you.
Ludwig	…My people? Turn against me?
Pfordten	This is an age of democratic whisperings, Sire. Of revolutions—and of coups. Should we wish to retain our power, we are all of us at the people's mercy. (*producing a paper order*)
Ludwig	You speak as though I had no choice.
Pfordten	The choice, of course, is His Majesty's alone.

After a long moment, Ludwig takes up a pen. He signs the order.

	Preparations have been made for your speech to the troops at the Kaiserhof.

Ludwig	There shall be no speech! I'll not be paraded before the public to promote the Confederation's vile and violent course. As far as I am concerned, this war is not happening. Richard!
Richard	Sire.
Ludwig	Ready the horses. We leave today as planned for the Alpsee.
Queen Mother	Your Majesty…
Ludwig	Oh. Mother.

He moves towards the Queen Mother, choking back tears, deeply moved.

	That we should live in such a century— When the will of a monarch might be so overruled!
Queen Mother	My King! The events of today are of no consequence. People, politics— These are none of your concerns! You must pay them no further heed. Your fate is greater.
Ludwig	Greater?
Queen Mother	Far greater! Yours is a duty which is sacred and dear!

Ludwig	Only guide me, as you did when I was a boy. Tell me what I must do.
Queen Mother	(*dreamily*) My King! You must wed! You must produce an heir!

He sinks into his mother's skirts. She stiffens, dismayed at this break in decorum.

Ludwig	You know, as well as I— I shall never wed. I shall never produce an heir. ... Mother, Have you heard me?
Queen Mother	Yes, My King. Yes. You shall wed. You shall produce an heir. And through you, the line shall continue! The House of Wittelsbach shall go on!

The Queen Mother pulls her skirts away from Ludwig. He stands. They exit together from the committee. Richard moves to follow; he's stopped in his tracks by Minister Pfordten.

Pfordten	He called you 'Richard.'
Richard	Excuse me?
Pfordten	The king. He called you 'Richard.'
Richard	What else should he call me?

Pfordten moves in close to Richard, who tenses.

Pfordten It is a *good* thing, Hornig, that you have earned the King's confidence. In fact, it is one of the very reasons I selected you for this post—

Pfordten takes Richard's face in his hand.

I seem to remember from our military days that currying favour with men in power is one of your particular talents.

Richard pulls away.

Richard You don't know what you're talking about.

Pfordten I know too well.
And now that you are in regular contact with the king –

Richard I'm here to run the stables, not to be your spy.

Pfordten Perhaps you've forgotten the state my men found you in before you were positioned so advantageously. Blind drunk in the early hours of some seedy drinking hall, numbed out of your senses, babbling to anyone who'd listen about another lost job, another time you *couldn't cope* –

Richard moves to exit.

Failing that, you remember the Schleswig-Holstein affair.

Richard Don't.

Pfordten The state you were in
After learning of the death of your friend,
Captain Ernst von Hess.
(nasty) The profanities, the obscene oaths
you declared –

Richard There was nothing dishonest between Ernst
and me –

Pfordten You know *damn well* where you'd be if I
hadn't intervened, it's a miracle you were
discharged so honourably.

Richard You know that I am grateful –

Pfordten So why am I playing catch up to the King's
sudden inclination to rule over matters of
State? I do not need my job made more
difficult than it already is running
interference on a fool figurehead who
suddenly thinks himself a ruler: who
undermines my *word*, my *influence*, my
authority as Minister at every turn!
…
You were always a good soldier, Hornig,
your – *indiscretions* – notwithstanding. I'm a
practical man. I understand that there's a
place for men like you. And now that you
have the King's confidence –

Richard I won't betray it.

Pfordten You already have.

Richard   I –

Pfordten   What should your new protector think, I wonder? To learn the terms by which you were placed here? To discover the *debt*, the *loyalty* you owe to one of his ministers? Why, with one word from me, I should think the king would never call you 'Richard' again . . .

He proffers a diary.

> From this moment,
> I want to know where he is,
> What he is doing,
> And with whom he is doing it.
> I want to know what he dreams,
> Dreads,
> Desires.

Richard takes the diary, slipping it into his coat pocket.

THE REIGNS

*A starry night, outside the steps to **Ludwig's summer palace** by the Alpsee. RICHARD sits alone on the steps, smoking a cigarette. LUDWIG enters from inside, releasing slamming dance music from within. He's sweaty, wearing a 17th century French courtiers' costume, with a golden sun mask.*

Ludwig	Aren't you enjoying the party?
Richard	Couldn't think in there.
Ludwig	That was your first mistake. Thinking.

He takes the cigarette from Richard, takes a drag, stands, jumps up and down a bit.

Richard	What are you doing now?
Ludwig	I'm trying to reach the stars!
	And Jupiter, and Mars, and Venus!
	The Moon!
	I spent every summer in this palace when I was young.
	I thought myself blessed,
	To be always surrounded by such beauty.
	The inky black sky dotted with silver stars,
	The crystal-clear waters of the Alpsee.
	I'd look up at the mountains,
	Sacred,
	Out of reach,
	and know nothing but –
	Possibility!
	Since I took the throne,
	Each year,

	My mother has desecrated this place with her prosaic presence, Has *desecrated* the gods and the celestial breezes! If she only knew how we were now employing her precious summer palace –
Richard	You shouldn't –
Ludwig	Why not?
Richard	Perhaps you shouldn't, With me, Share Anything so intimate, personal –
Ludwig	I see.
Richard	No –
Ludwig	You're right, of course, We could never – not *really*—we –

He covers his face with his hands. He moans.

> OH…

Richard stands. He embraces Ludwig, who sobs into his shoulder.

> Richard, we mustn't allow it—
> I can't afford to lose it again!

Richard	To lose—?
Ludwig	My sovereignty! I can't afford to lose it. Not in the next reign.

55

Richard The next reign. And this is…?

Ludwig The fifth.
(*indicating his costume*)
Louis the Fourteenth, the Sun King, was first.
Louis the Fifteenth, the Well-Beloved, second.
Louis the Sixteenth, Restorer of Liberty, third.
Louis the Seventeenth, poor wretch, was nipped in the bud by Revolution!
Louis the Eighteenth, the Desired, my grandfather's godfather, was fourth!
And fifth is –

Richard Ludwig the Second?

Ludwig Ludwig.
Louis.
Can't you see?
…
You think that I am mad.

Richard I don't.

Ludwig Richard, there are things I wish to say.

Richard I want you to say them.

Ludwig Things I wish to share with you.

Richard You're not listening.

Ludwig I –

Richard kisses Ludwig.

Richard I do.

NEUSCHWANSTEIN

Day breaks, as LUDWIG and RICHARD hike up a hill by the Alpsee. Ludwig stops to observe the ruins of a castle.

Richard   It's not what I expected, it's—

Ludwig   Ruins.
In the middle ages,
A great fortress stood atop this hill.
The knights who lived here—
They didn't make their fame through bloodshed, or deeds of service.
But through song.
They were Minnesänger, renowned for their skill at singing courtly songs of love.
Here, high halls once echoed their love songs, soft and sweet.
…
My father, when he repaired our summer palace along the Alpsee, has its halls painted with scenes of legendary knights.
As a boy, I'd wander those halls and feel myself transported to a strange, distant past.
To a place of awe-inspired, heroic beauty.
I'd look up,
Here,
At the ruins of the Swan Stone and I'd see…

Richard   What did you see?

Ludwig   Nothing, Richard.
Ruins.

Richard I don't believe you.

Richard moves to touch Ludwig, who prickles, resisting.

You dreamed something.

Ludwig I dreamed many things, none of them any more than a child's fancies!
…
You ask me what I see?
I see—
A machine.
A perfect machine,
Efficient and ruthless.
Oiled to mobilize,
To subordinate,
To raze,
To wrest,
To ruin.
I see,
An age, which is faster,
Sleeker,
Meaner.
A people
Fed by hatred,
Suspicion,
Greed.
A World,
Raped
And
Racing to its own extinction.
Its soul starved of magic,
Music,

>   Mystery,
>   Anathema to
>   Beauty,
>   Art,
>   Romance.
>   I see technology,
>   Industry,
>   Accelerating with endless momentum,
>   Acceleration,
>   An end to its own means.
>   There is no place for dreams here.
>   There is only metal,
>   Cold,
>   Precise,
>   and the body,
>   spirit,
>   mind of Man,
>   left broken beneath it—

Richard   So make a new world.

Ludwig   They will not allow it.

Richard   The likes of which you spoke before the committee.

Ludwig   They will not allow me to –

Richard   Do not ask them!

Richard tackles Ludwig: they struggle against one another amidst the ruins.

Ludwig   You are mad!

Richard	HAH.
Ludwig	Mad!
Richard	You brought me to this place, Here To this place
Ludwig	Which once was more!
Richard	And might it not be? More! If someone raised it?
Ludwig	Where?
Richard	There!

Richard releases Ludwig. He gazes up.

	Just there. Rising, From rubble to sky. Out of time, And place
Ludwig	What is it?
Richard	A tower! Rising up, Out of reach, Up, to touch the (?)
Ludwig	Clouds?
Richard	No! Higher!

	To touch the Heavens!
Ludwig	You really are mad.
Richard	But can't you see it!? Rising, Higher! As if from a dream, A dream made real, A dream made from— stone. A fortress, made from walls of stone, strong, solid.

Richard moves close, wrapping his arms about Ludwig.

	A fortress. Out of reach.
Ludwig	No one gets in.
Richard	Or out.
Ludwig	And within?
Richard	Within—? A room. A vast hall.
Ludwig	In gold and ivory Beset with pillar upon pillar of porphyry and lapis lazuli.
Richard	And above—
Ludwig	A great dome, Bright blue as the firmament, gold as the sun and stars.

	Beneath it –
Richard	A throne.
Ludwig	No.
Richard	No throne?
Ludwig	A dais. Left empty. As in Parsifal's grail hall. An empty place.

Richard turns to face Ludwig, steamy, intense.

Richard   A promise.

NEW WORLD (pt. 1)

Months later. **A construction site at Linderhof.** *An ARCHITECT consults plans and papers with RICHARD H.*

Architect	A grotto? In the middle of the Bavarian countryside? Erecting a 17th century petit palais amidst the Alps is one thing – all those rose-arbours – the fountains – But this?
Richard H	The king requires a grotto.
Architect	We shall have to carve into the rock-face!
Richard H	Then carve.
Architect	Even so, if it's to hold water –
Richard H	An artificial lake, with a running waterfall. It will need to produce waves, for the boat.
Architect	I assure you the king will not wish to enter cold water pumped in from the Alpsee.
Richard H	Will it be cold? That won't do.
Architect	What do you suggest, we carve into the bedrock and install furnaces!?
Richard H	And we'll need a light show. Bright, coloured lights, in rotating sequences, Pink Purple Yellow Cerulean
Architect	Anything *else?*

Richard H	(*consulting his notes*) 'A long, velvet rope which, once pulled, shall activate the appearance of a glimmering rainbow.'
Architect	Sir, I must *insist* on speaking to the king.
Richard H	The king will not wish to speak to yet another inept architect who fails to grasp his vision. He hasn't hesitated to quickly dispatch those before you, so unless you'd like to go the same way, I'd stop asking questions and start finding solutions.
Architect	Very well. A – a rainbow.

The Architect exits with his plans. LUDWIG enters in a dressing gown, wielding a pile of letters.

Ludwig	Another pile from the minister!
Richard H	Don't bother with those.
Ludwig	(*eyeing the ink through the envelope*) His appeals grow more fevered by the day. Perhaps I ought to answer…

Richard snatches and pockets the letters.

Richard H	You're here to get away from the court, not to be hounded by your ministers.
Ludwig	What would I do without you, Richard?

He presses Ludwig up against the gritty cement wall.

Richard H	I have something for you.

Ludwig	I know you do.
Malvina	(*offstage*) Bloody hell, it's gorgeous as tits out here!

WAGNER and his Prima Donna, MALVINA, appear, in full medieval costumes, a la 'Tristan & Isolde'.

Ludwig	Herr Wagner!
Wagner	My King!
Richard H	What is he doing here?
Wagner	Malvina. The cup.

Malvina hands Wagner a golden chalice: Wagner presents it to Ludwig.

	Thought we'd make a good start to your birthday weekend, my King. This stuff's been illegal on order of death since the Holy Roman Empire wiped out the Eleusinian mysteries.
Ludwig	I never dreamed my invitation would move the Friend so swiftly, not in the midst of his rehearsals!
Wagner	And he's brought you a gift. (*presenting Malvina*) Your Isolde.
Ludwig	Isolde!!
Malvina	My King. My *Liege*.

Wagner (*indicating the site*) How quickly your project progresses.

Ludwig But this is nothing!
Only wait until you see our plans to resurrect the desecrated swan stone—
A knightly fortress,
Sacred,
Out of reach,
A worthy temple for the divine Friend.

Richard H pulls Ludwig aside.

Richard H I thought we'd have Linderhof to ourselves.

Ludwig As did I!
(*off Richard's look*) You're upset. Oh, Richard. I promise you, this weekend – it is still ours.
You and he, you'll get along. I know you will! Say you'll try.

Wagner I downed a cup of that stuff an hour ago and I swear to Jewish-Judas there are little Nibelungen trying to escape from under my skin.

Malvina Let's take a swim. Naked! In the Alpsee!

Wagner and Malvina run off. Ludwig lifts the chalice to Richard H's lips.

Ludwig My King.

After a moment, Richard H drinks from it. Wagnerian leitmotif: 'Longing, Desire'.

UNDER DER LINDEN

*WAGNER and MALVINA swim in **the Alpsee**. Wagner plucks a lute, Malvina sings 'Under Der Linden'. Throughout her song: LUDWIG pulls RICHARD H to the shore. Ludwig wades into the water. Richard H, surrounded by discarded medieval costumes, reaches down, takes up a swan helmet (a la Wagner's 'Lohengrin'), places it on his head. He watches from the shore as Ludwig frolics with the composer and his star.*

Malvina   *(singing)*

Under der Linden	*[Under the Linden*
An der Heide,	*On the heather,*
Dâ unser zweier Bette was:	*Where we shared a place of rest:*
Dâ muget ir vinden,	*Still you may find there,*
Schône beide,	*Lovely together,*
Gebrochen Bluomen unde Gras.	*Flowers crushed and grass down-pressed.*
Vor dem walde in einem tal,	*Beside the forest in the vale,*
Tandaradei,	*Tandaradei,*
Schône sanc diu nahtegal.	*Sweetly sang the nightingale.]*
Ich kam gegangen	*[I came to meet him*
Zuo der ouwe:	*At the green:*
Dô was mîn friedel komen ê.	*There was my true love come before.*
Dâ wart ich empfangen	*Such was I greeted –*
Hêre frouwe	*Heaven's Queen! –*
Daz ich bin sælic iemer mê.	*That I am glad for evermore.*
Kust er mich? wol tûsentstunt:	*Had he kisses? A thousand some:*
Tandaradei,	*Tandaradei,*
Seht wie rôt mir ist der munt.	*See how red my mouth's become.]*
Dô hete er gemachet,	*[There he had fashioned,*
Alsô rîche,	*For luxury,*

Von Bluomen eine Bettestat.	*A bed from every kind of flower.*
Des wirt noch gelachet	*It sets to laughing,*
Innecliche,	*Delightedly,*
Kumt iemen an daz selbe pfat.	*Whoever comes upon that bower;*
Bî den rôsen er wol mac,	*By the roses well one may,*
Tandaradei,	*Tandaradei,*
Merken wâ mirz houbet lac.	*Mark the spot my head once lay.]*
Daz er bî mir læge,	*[If any knew,*
Wesse ez iemen	*He lay with me*
(Nu enwelle Got!),	*(May God forbid!),*
so schamte ich mich.	*for shame I'd die.*
Wes er mit mir pflæge,	*What did he do?*
Niemer niemen	*May none but he*
Bevinde daz wan er und ich	*Ever be sure of that – and I*
Und ein kleinez Vogellîn:	*And one extremely tiny bird,*
tandaradei,	*Tandaradei,*
daz mac wol getriuwe sîn.	*Who will, I think, not say a word.]*

BAD WAGNER

*Later that night. RICHARD H stumbles, drunken, perhaps humming the tune, into the **stables**. He stifles his surprise, then spies on WAGNER and MALVINA, in cotton undergarments, entwined upon bales of hay.*

Malvina But Maestro – !

Wagner Malvina!

He buries his face in her bust.

Malvina What should my husband, Herr Schnorr – your Tristan! – think? To see his Maestro so disposed!

Wagner (*coming up for air*) It is only natural a Maestro must discover the depth of his star's talent.

Malvina (*dazzled*) His star?

Wagner And how should you think to sing my 'Isolde,'

Malvina gasps, as Wagner reaches up her skirts.

Before having received proper musical instruction.

Malvina But – in the stables at Linderhof – what of the king?

Wagner What?
The Boy Wonder?
The Child Sovereign?

	Who has abandoned all duties but the construction of his every mad fancy? Dear woman, I assure you, you needn't worry about him.
Malvina	(*gasping in pleasure*) Oh!
Wagner	As sure as you now tremble, Agitated to the point of blind ecstasy at my touch, The Fairy Tale King is mere putty in my hands. Whatever I ask of him, it must be mine. Whether money, Property, Fame, He must supply it. And for the price of a song. Little Ludwig. My Boy. He shall build me my opera house, A veritable temple at the shore of the Isar River. Within it, The name of Richard Wagner shall be enshrined forever. From its halls, It shall echo throughout the world! It is there, dear Nightingale, That you shall be my star –

Malvina sings out, hitting a powerful high note.

Spotlight *on Richard H: he removes Minister Pfordten's diary and letters from his coat pocket.*

Richard H   Mister Pfordten.
   I'm ready to speak.

Pfordten   (*appearing in **spot***) So, speak.

FROM HENCEFORTH NEVER

LUDWIG and MALVINA sit on a rug in Ludwig's 'Moorish Kiosk', sipping tea and wearing bits of the various Wagnerian costume pieces strewn about: a winged helmet, Viking horns, plates of armour, etc.

Malvina Your Highness,
Last night I dreamt the most fantastic dream.

Ludwig (*pouring tea for Malvina*)
You must tell me at once, Princess!

Malvina How fantastic it was! I dreamt I came out of a beautiful wood into a rolling green meadow, in the middle of which stood a large, handsome lion.

Ludwig A lion?

Malvina A lion, surrounded on all sides by tigers and hyenas! The noble lion, he only surveyed these deceitful creatures, full of contempt – when, suddenly, they fell upon him, tearing at him! Murder! With a cry of rage, I fell upon the lion so that the cowardly killers drew back, and, after a second cry, fled hastily from the woods!

She downs her tea, delighted with herself. Ludwig takes the cup from her, studies its tea leaves.

Ludwig The lion – it is the symbol on my crest.

Wagner (*off-stage*) My King!

WAGNER barges into the room, newspaper in hand,
RICHARD H holding him back.

Richard H   He is not to be disturbed this way –

Wagner   (*breaking loose*)
There must be hell paid!
There must be heads on GODDAMN spikes!

Richard H   Sire –

Wagner   My King!
The Munich presses,
They must be stopped.
They go too far –

Richard H   This is neither the time nor place.

Wagner   For the last time,
They have libelled my character,
Disgraced my name!

Ludwig   (*taking the paper*) Come, Friend, it is never as bad as you say.

Wagner   It is worse! They have branded me an –

Ludwig   (*impressed*) '…amoral charlatan…'
there's some blood in that!

Wagner   They have spread salacious rumours about my relationship with Frau von Bülow (my conductor's wife!), about the propriety of my conduct with dear Malvina, my own Isolde—

Ludwig   '…Herr Wagner's prodigious fornications…'

Malvina Oh!

Wagner They have cast aspersions upon my artistry, my moral fibre, my political integrity as an anti-capitalist!

Ludwig Is your annual stipend really *twelve* times that of the average Munich citizen?

Wagner Curs! Philistines! They must be publicly punished, pilloried for their vicious lies!

Ludwig They know about the opera house.

Wagner …Sire?

Ludwig They have details, *accurate* details about the opera house, they have numbers and figures no one outside the royal house has access to. Yet you say they lie?

Richard H Can't this wait until we've returned to the city?

Wagner Your Highness –

Ludwig (*standing*) They have said you regard your royal patron as little more than a 'glorified creditor.'

Wagner And you believe them!?

Ludwig Herr Wagner—

Wagner And so, does the whole world turn at once against me?
Must I never see my great work flourish?

> The entirety of my life's labour, beset on all sides by bloodthirsty villains!
> A Munich public too imbecilic to receive true music –
> a mechanical, greasepaint nineteenth century theatre too DEAD to breathe life into my art –
> a JEW conductor who fumbles barbarously through my score, baton slashing through the air with all the poetry of a swine devouring a trough of rancid slop!
> I have held my tongue thus far,
> have rubbed ash in the wound,
> but now,
> shall I lie down and allow the presses,
> those Bavarian BUTCHERS,
> to smother my opera house at its inception?
> It is too much for one man to bear,
> it is MUCH TOO MUCH.

They stare at Wagner, who comes back to himself, as if from a fever dream.

> Your Highness, I...

Ludwig You may be glad, Friend.
> They shall no longer disgrace your good name.
> *(to Richard H)*
> Send word to my Council of Ministers—
> From henceforth, Herr Wagner is not to set foot on Bavarian soil.

Wagner But Sire!

Malvina   To be exiled!

Richard H   Are you sure—?

Ludwig   From henceforth, never!

SWITZERLAND

LUDWIG sits at the shore of the Alpsee, staring into the water, like Caravaggio's 'Narcissus'. RICHARD moves to approach, hesitates, hovers.

Ludwig   I have failed them.
My people
My country
My family

Richard   You have tried – for their sake – to help them.

Ludwig   At everything I have tried, I have failed.

Richard   You haven't failed.

Ludwig   At some point – how did it happen? – I left them.
And perhaps, because—
They don't need me.

Richard   I need you.

Ludwig   So, let's do it.

Richard   Let's – ?

Ludwig   Leave this.
All of it.

Richard   Your Kingdom?

Ludwig   I'll abdicate.

Richard   You'll—

Ludwig	Renounce the throne! And all its barren splendour.
Richard	You have told your ministers you'll open parliament in May.
Ludwig	Why should I? If my government will deny me sovereignty, let Minister Pfordten do the honour.
Richard	You're not serious.
Ludwig	Why not? You don't believe me.
Richard	It doesn't matter. Wherever you go, I shall follow.
Ludwig	Even to Switzerland?
Richard	Even to Switzerland.
Ludwig	To Lucerne. That's where we'll go. Somewhere secluded. Under the blue shadow of the Swiss Alps, We'll build a cabin.
Richard	Already putting me to work, are you?
Ludwig	I'd help!
Richard	Even in your daydreams.
Ludwig	I'd – you know – hammer joists –
Richard	That I'd like to see.

Ludwig	Who says it's a daydream? … We'll build a cabin.
Richard	And chop wood.
Ludwig	And sit by the fire every night. No one will know us there.
Richard	And no one will care.
Ludwig	No more people or politics. No state, no religion.
Richard	No more anyone, Anything else.
Ludwig	Only Switzerland. And the mountains. And in the distance— *(as if hearing it)* Music.
Richard	Music?
Ludwig	Music! Sweeping music! For we are in Tribchen, And just up the path from the woods is the villa of The Friend, And each day we come to pay our tribute, To be cast adrift on the sea of his music!

Richard pulls away.

Richard	You mean Wagner?

Ludwig Certainly.

Richard After everything he's said and done, how could you ever—?

Ludwig Oh. Richard.
It's all new to you, I know, but this is the way it is with great artists.

Richard You banished him, ordered him into exile.

Ludwig What choice did I have? You see how they have turned on him! The people of Munich will never accept Wagner. I must be sure he never sets foot here, not until the world knows him for the genius he is. His work must be free to develop, unhindered, must be allowed to live on –

Richard Surely you won't still provide him funds.

Ludwig I shall provide him whatever he needs.

Richard After the way he's abused you!

Ludwig Herr Wagner is a complicated man.

Richard He is a vampire!

Ludwig He has given my life its meaning.

Richard He would take your life from you without thinking twice!

Ludwig It is a small price to pay! For work that shall live forever!

Richard   You cannot forgive him.

Ludwig   Richard.

Richard   You must not.
                If you knew how he truly regarded you,
                How he mocks you—
                Under your nose
                (In your palace)
                To scheme to exploit you,
                To demean you with pet names,
                To call you his 'boy' –

Ludwig   'His boy'?

Richard   What?

Ludwig   How do you—
                To call me his 'boy'?
                How do you know that he—

Ludwig moves away.

                They had—
                Richard, they had numbers, figures,
                They had –

Richard   It's not what you think.

Ludwig   Tell me you didn't.

Richard   I –

Ludwig   Say you didn't.

Richard   Only for your sake—
                Only to—

Ludwig   Who did you?

Richard   Let me explain

Ludwig   Minister Pfordten?
                   Did you – ?
                   Have you – ?
                   Oh
                   God.

Richard   I only did what had to be done to *protect* you.

Ludwig   DON'T TOUCH ME.
                   I don't need your protection, Richard!
                   I don't need you to save me. I am not Ernst.

Richard   That's not –
                   That isn't –

Ludwig   Do you really believe you did this for me?
                   If you believed in me,
                   My vision—

Richard   Neuschwanstein.
                   Is that the vision you mean?
                   Your tribute to him.
                   Sacred,
                   Out of reach.

Ludwig   Jealousy.
                   Is that what this is?
                   When my largess benefitted you, you had nothing to say of it, but now? I could have gone all my life never knowing an emotion so base.

	so *utterly* common.
	It's as they say, then: if you lie with *dogs*—
Richard	Pathetic.
Ludwig	You would dare?
Richard	You would dare!
	YOU would dare!
	When *I* am the one
	who holds your hand,
	On nights you cannot sleep,
	And tells you the voices are in your head.
	When you roll against me in your sleep,
	And grasp me so tightly,
	I think sometimes you're afraid I'll vanish into thin air.
	Holding me,
	Muttering,
	'This is real,
	This is real'
	so afraid,
	that if you let me go you might cease to exist.
	I am here.
	Now.
	THIS is real.
	And still,
	you choose to be lied to
	to live a fantasy
	with no regard for whether you live or die
	When I would do anything
	ANYTHNG

>					to keep you safe.
>					and you believe you don't need my protection?
>					You really must be crazy.
>					As fucking
>					MENTAL
>					as they all say

Ludwig   Go.

Richard   So that's it,
               you'd banish me too?
               Please –
               Ludwig.

Ludwig   You disgust me.
               You
               DISGUST ME
               DOG
               PEASANT
               GO

Ludwig brandishes his sword. Richard removes a ring, throws it at Ludwig's feet, exits.

NEW WORLD (pt. 2)

*The scaffolded site of **Neuschwanstein**. LUDWIG sabres a bottle of champagne, pours it over his lips, chin, chest. Thumping music.*

Ludwig Crack.
The sound of
Metal spikes on stones,
Now
Chiselled smooth,
Round and gleaming.
Smooth stones,
Lifted,
Stacked,
Cemented into thick walls.
Entombed.
Stones,
stacked and spackled one by one into
spiralling stairwells,
Leading up to nothing but—
Stones
lifted
in grey dust hands
black and
Sooty.
Stacked higher and
Higher—
Stacked,
Into passages,
Long
and
Winding.

Halls which have been
Smeared
and
Plastered
Painted
and
Gilt with gold.
A hall of mirrors,
Long
and
Empty
An unfinished wing
Leading to
Rooms,
Closed off,
forgotten.
Never to be used.

MINISTER PFORDTEN and the QUEEN MOTHER appear in spots.

Pfordten   Your Highness—

Queen Mother   I am told he sees no one.
I am told,
Even his servants are made to avert their eyes as they pass him in the halls.

Ludwig   They must be completed.

Pfordten   Another line of credit is out of the question.

Ludwig   Then I shall go above you.

Pfordten   Your Council of Ministers will not allow it.

Ludwig	THEN I SHALL REPLACE THEM ALL!
Queen Mother	I am told, He keeps only the company of strangers, That he is a stranger to his kind. Most meals, He eats on his own, In the study at Linderhof, A table raised up and down on pulleys through the floor.

RICHARD appears, stacking bales of hay at the stable of a peasant's cottage in Füssen.

Richard	For a while, I obey you. I take anonymous work where I can find it. I work in stables, Rough up my hands.
Ludwig	Smooth stones stacked by grey soot hands
Richard	When people speak of you, They speak as if you were myth.
Queen Mother	I am told, Under moonlight He rides on a silver sledge through the snow. He removes rings and trinkets from his slender fingers. Dispenses gold from a silver purse.
Richard	I begin to think,

	It's true.
	That somehow, I have conjured you.
Pfordten	There is more
	Madam—
Ludwig	Always more.
	More air more colour more music more light
	Bigger
	Brighter
	Bolder
	MORE
Pfordten	We have tried,
	As best we could.
Queen Mother	We have tried.
Pfordten	But the truth
	I'm afraid,
	Is all too clear.
	And now that he has threatened to overturn his council…
	I suggest we speak to Doctor von Gudden—
Queen Mother	But Sir!
	He is still our King!
Pfordten	He is a danger.
	To himself,
	To others.
Queen Mother	But Sir –
Pfordten	What they have told you,
	Madam,

	Is true.
	But there is more—
Ludwig	Sooty fingers
	Touching chest
	Soft skin
	Gripped
	Rough,
	and
	Hard
	Like stone.
	Under moonlight,
	Flesh,
	The scent of sweat
	And strangers
	Their taste.
	Pine-needles pressed into the backs of knees.
Pfordten	I should spare you the testimonies,
	But rest assured,
	They are legion.
Ludwig	In their arms,
	Enfolded,
	Enraptured,
	Ravished over bare palace floors,
	Again,
	and
	Again,
	and Again
	Always more
	Ever charging
	More,

                        Until each has had their fill,
                        More air more colour more music more light
                        Bigger
                        Brighter
                        Bolder
                        MORE

Queen Mother   ENOUGH.
                        ...
                        We have tried.
                        He is a danger.
                        To himself.
                        To others.
                        We have tried, and now—

Pfordten   I'll send for Doctor von Gudden.

Exeunt, then:

MINISTER PFORDTEN stands at the entry to the stable at Füssen, cornering RICHARD.

Pfordten   You're one slippery bastard, Hornig.

Richard   Why are you here?

Pfordten   I have another job for you.

Richard   ...

Pfordten   Nothing like that. I'm about to be much raised in stature in this court, and I'll need my best men close at hand.

Richard   He doesn't trust you enough to make you Prime Minister.

Pfordten	It no longer matters whom he trusts, or favours. You'll find, with a deposed monarch, such whims are suddenly unimportant.
Richard	The people would never depose him.
Pfordten	They needn't. Not after he's been declared mentally unfit to rule. And, after all, you supplied some of our doctors' favourite bits of testimony.
Richard	BASTARD.

Richard slams Pfordten up against a wall.

Pfordten Stand down,
Hornig!
You forget yourself!
You forget
I own you!
You belong to me!

Richard releases Pfordten. He runs.

RUN

*Rain pours, as RICHARD runs through the **countryside**.*

Richard My lungs burn as I race across the countryside,
Gasping,
Desperate through the darkness,
beating against the pummelling rain.
My mind is muddled,
Moving faster than my feet can carry me—
I stumble,
fall –
Crash hard into the mud.

I look up at the sky.
Looking up, at all that great black vastness,
I feel suddenly small, impossibly small.

I imagine then,
how it might feel.
To let go.
Finally.
To finally stop fighting.
To surrender to it.
To all that great, black vastness.

Sound of Wagnerian Horns.

Only – it's then, that –
This moment.

The light of blazing torches begins to fill the stage.

Torches.
Shouts.
Bodies.
Pushing hard through the night,
Gathered in the rain from surrounding villages.
Your people.

Pushing hard, towards the fabled keep of their Dream King.
Your people.
They're shouting for you.
They're calling your name.
A revolt.
Against this coup.
They're calling –
'Ludwig! Ludwig!'

And as the flames of their torches fill the darkness,
My eyes catch sight of something.
High up, in the distance.
Something,
Revealed only fleetingly, from the road, crossing the gorge below.

Ludwig appears, elevated in heroic tableau, bathed in light.

A castle.
There.
Rising up, out of time and place.
A tower of white stone,
Out of reach,
Rising higher,

>To touch the heavens.
>Rising,
>As if from a dream.
>A dream made real.
>A dream made from stone.

Light on Ludwig dims.

>I stand, to raise myself up,
>Up out of the mud.
>The smell of licking flames,
>the sound of gathering masses,
>Vivid colours, bright, shimmering.
>I look up,
>Once more,
>And though the image has gone…
>The way forward is clear.
>I run.

COME WITH ME

*RICHARD has climbed **the tower** at Neuschwanstein. LUDWIG stands dangerously close to the ledge of its lookout.*

Ludwig   It is done.

Richard   No.

Ludwig   They're at the gate. With four doctors, doctors I've never met, ready to swear that I, Ludwig II, King of Bavaria, have gone utterly, irreparably mad.

Richard   Come down from there.

Ludwig   Well – haven't I?

Richard   Don't believe it.

Ludwig   After all, perhaps I have.

Richard moves closer to the ledge.

Richard   Come with me.

Ludwig   Where?

Richard   To Munich.

Ludwig   I can't breathe the air in Munich.

Richard   To Switzerland, then.

Ludwig   What should we do in Switzerland?

Richard   Nothing.

Ludwig   I do miss the smell of it there.

Richard	The air. The mountains.
Ludwig	And all this . . .?
Richard	We leave it behind. All of it. Everything. No more anyone, Anything else. Just us.
Ludwig	Under the blazing sun and stars.
Richard	Ludwig.
Ludwig	Richard, I—

Suddenly, there is torchlight, shouting from below.

Richard	Don't –
Ludwig	They're calling my name.
Richard	Don't go.
Ludwig	But they're calling my name!
Richard	Stay.
Ludwig	I can't.
Richard	But –
Ludwig	I can't run. You know that I can't. I never could. Not really. Switzerland— it was only ever a dream. You know as well as I.

Richard   But couldn't it be real?

Ludwig   One day.
                Perhaps.
                Perhaps,
                In the next reign.

Richard   They'll imprison you.

Ludwig   Yes.

Richard   They'll say you were mad.

Ludwig   Yes.

Richard   And if they do worse?
                If they kill you?

                If they find you,
                Three days from now,
                Here,
                At the shore of Lake Starnberg,
                Floating face down in shallow water—
                Signs of a struggle,
                Next to the body of your committing doctor.

                If they erect a cross at the place of your death,
                A plain wooden cross,
                Rising up from the shore.

Ludwig   Richard –

Richard joins Ludwig at the ledge.

Richard   I'll follow.

Ludwig   If I should die—

Richard   Please.

Ludwig   You'll live.

Richard   I can't.

Ludwig   You'll live.

Richard   How can I?

Ludwig kisses Richard.

Ludwig   Your king commands it.

EPILOGUE

*At the shore of **Lake Starnberg**. QUEEN MOTHER and the PRIEST return. RICHARD removes the diary from his jacket pocket. He places it by the shore of the lake. He takes up a discarded flower from the shore, stands, places the flower in his lapel. He follows the procession off.*

The lake becomes suffused with golden light. Wagnerian Leitmotif: 'Genesis.'

End